Transcending the Fictive Dream with the Elements

Paul Cunningham

ISBN
Hardcover: 978-1-966902-14-0
Paperback: 978-1-966902-13-3

I'd like to thank the Spring Street Gallery on Block Island, the Block Island Public Library, the town of Block Island, and the open-minded students who dropped by for the opportunity to teach classes about the five elements and how they interact with art and narrative. To them I am forever grateful.

Contents

About the Author

I've had three screenplays optioned, a stack of poems published, and bylines in newspapers and magazines where the ink still smells like deadlines. My work rides the edge between the elemental and the unexpected—whether it's exploring the ghost-scars of a 1970s Kansas City gang war for an upcoming TV pilot, cooking up a Hitchcockian short where cannibalism is on the menu (but nobody talks about it), or carving out a dark romantic survival story that only pretends to be about love.

Mostly, I write because stories are how we survive—because the world breaks often, and narrative is one of the few tools sharp enough to shape meaning from the rubble.

I believe the best writing starts in the bones and burns through the skin. And I'm just here to follow that fire wherever it leads.

Introduction: Entering the Fictive Dream

Crickets and locusts are the squeaky wheels of summer. Guards are selling explosives to the patients. Things are really tricky.

And here you are.

Okay, the fictive dream. What are we talking about here? Let's start by saying that storytelling isn't just words on a page or scenes on a screen—it's a **process**, a movement, a force. It doesn't care about perfect grammar or carefully structured outlines. It sneaks up on you in the middle of the night, rides shotgun in your subconscious, waits in the wings while you're washing dishes or staring blankly at a wall. And here's the thing: you don't have to be some grand, omniscient authority to step into it. I'm not here to be your professor. I'm just a step ahead, cutting a path through the underbrush, waving you forward.

Two Threads of Inspiration

There are two ways stories show up. One is the **big blast**—the lightning strike, the idea that emerges fully formed like it's been cooking in the depths of your subconscious for years. You wake up, and *boom*, there it is. No warning, no negotiation, just raw, pulsing clarity demanding to be put on the page.

I remember the first time it happened to me. I'd been a poet, a prose writer, a halfhearted novelist, but never a screenwriter. Then I got injured. Stuck in a chair. Days stretched long and uneventful, and I did the only thing I could: watched movies. Let them soak into my bloodstream. And one day, the story **just appeared**—fully formed, like I'd been carrying it my whole life. With the help of a producer friend, I got it into screenplay form. It was **optioned in Hollywood, lived in development limbo, and then vanished**—because that's how the industry works sometimes. But the moment of inspiration? That was real. That was something undeniable.

Then there's the **other kind of inspiration**, the kind that doesn't hit all at once. The kind where you just **start walking**—following a thread, chasing a character, exploring a theme, sketching a scene. You don't know where it's leading. You don't know if it'll even turn into anything. But you follow it anyway.

This is where most stories actually come from—not from divine intervention, but from **movement**, from putting one foot in front of the other. Some people start with a character. Some start with a feeling. Some start at the end and reverse engineer their way back to the beginning. **It doesn't matter where you start as long as you start.**

I spent years bouncing between conflicting advice from writing books, trying to figure out why one thing worked, and another didn't. The real answer? **There is no single right way.** But when I started looking at storytelling the way I had learned to look at martial arts, healing work, at **the elements**, it finally made sense. The Earth, Water, Fire, Wind, and Void—each one a different force in the creative process.

This is the essence of the **fictive dream**—where the story isn't just a structure but a living, shifting thing growing in rhythm with nature itself.

Shaking Up the Status Quo

Traditional storytelling methods like to pretend they've got it all figured out. Three-act structures. Beat sheets. Save the Cat. Maybe those work for some people. But I don't trust any system that **pretends the wind doesn't blow.**

If you've ever stepped outside on a stormy day, you know that **nature doesn't move in straight lines.** A river carves its own path. Fire burns unpredictably. Wind shifts without warning. This is how stories should move—**not like a checklist, but like a force of nature.**

So, let's throw out the rulebook. Ask yourself:

- *How do stories shape us?*

- *How can we reshape them?*

- *Where does the real energy live—not the formulaic, pre-packaged beats, but the **pulse** of a story?*

We're not here to build a rigid framework. We're here to **discover how narrative moves,** how it morphs, how it breathes. **The goal isn't control. The goal is understanding.**

A Roadmap Through the Elements

We'll explore **five elemental forces,** each representing a different creative stage and emotional polarity:

- **Earth** – The foundation. The world, the characters, the structure. But Earth isn't just stable—it also holds **the potential for disruption,** for sudden fractures that change everything.

- **Water** – The emotional undercurrent. Intuition, flow, uncertainty. Water is the **ebb and flow of creative energy**—sometimes clear, sometimes murky, always moving.

- **Fire** – Passion, obsession, ignition. The spark that turns into an inferno. Fire **drives a story forward**, but it can also burn everything to the ground if unchecked.

- **Wind** – The force of change. Unpredictable, uncontainable, sweeping ideas in from unexpected places. Wind is what takes a static idea and turns it into something **alive**.

- **The Void** – The place where everything **comes together and falls apart**. Full synthesis and early signs of decay, all at once. This is where stories **find their shape— or unravel**.

Each of these elements has a polarity. Stability vs. disruption. Clarity vs. confusion. Passion vs. obsession. Love vs. fixation. **A story moves through these polarities, whether you recognize it or not.**

Some of you will feel at home on Earth—building solid worlds and crafting structured narratives. Others will live in Fire, chasing themes, characters, and wild arcs of emotion. Some of you will jump straight to the Void and work backward, writing toward a single moment of meaning.

It doesn't matter where you begin. It only matters that you do.

Breaking Through Creative Blocks

Most creative blocks happen because we **get stuck in one element too long.**

Maybe you're too rooted in Earth—your worldbuilding is airtight, but nothing moves. Maybe you're drowning in Water, lost in emotional depth with no sense of direction. Maybe Fire has taken over, and the obsession is burning a hole in your story. Maybe the Wind is too chaotic, blowing you in a hundred directions at once. Maybe the Void has swallowed you whole, and the meaning of your work is **disintegrating before your eyes.**

The solution? Move. Shift elements. **Disrupt yourself.**

I once heard Robert Bly say, *"Your poems have already been written. They just don't trust you enough to come out yet."* That stuck with me. Your stories are already inside you. The elements **are already in motion.** You just have to stop resisting them.

The Journey Ahead

This isn't a step-by-step manual. It's a **map**—a guide to walking through the elements, feeling their forces at work in your writing, **learning to follow their rhythms instead of forcing your own.**

We'll start with **Earth**, where stories take shape, where structures are built, where foundations are laid. And then, like all things in nature, we'll watch that foundation shift.

The wind is rising. The fire flickers. The water is restless.

The fictive dream is waiting.

Let's begin.

Chapter 1: Earth – The Grounding Force

Crickets and locusts are the squeaky wheels of summer. Guards are selling explosives to the patients. Things are really tricky.

And yet, the earth holds.

When I talk about the fictive dream, I'm not speaking of some ethereal, far-off plane where ideas drift like smoke, impossible to catch. I'm talking about something solid—**pulse-driven, bone-deep, like the weight of dirt in your hands, like the floor beneath your feet.**

Storytelling starts here. Not in the flash of inspiration. Not in the fire of obsession. Not in the wind of a new idea blowing in at just the right moment. **It starts in the ground.**

Two Threads of Inspiration: The Slow Build and the Sudden Blast

There are two ways creativity arrives. One is **the sudden explosion,** the seismic shift where something long-buried in your subconscious cracks open and **demands to be written down now before it vanishes.**

I've felt it before. When I was younger, I was laid up with an injury—nothing to do but sit, watch movies, and let my brain soak in whatever it could. One day, **a story just hit.** Fully formed, like it had been waiting in the shadows for the right moment to step into the light. It was raw, autobiographical, real. I barely had to touch it— just transcribe what was already there. With the help of a producer friend, it became a screenplay. It was optioned. And then it fizzled. Hollywood swallowed it whole and left nothing but dust in its place.

The point? **Inspiration doesn't care what happens after it arrives. It only cares that you listen.**

Then there's the **other way**—the slow, patient journey of **building something from nothing.** This is Earth's domain. The steady accumulation of details, **laying down bricks one by one, even when you don't know what you're building yet.**

It's the difference between being struck by lightning and learning how to make fire with your bare hands.

The Dual Nature of Earth: Stability, Bread Crumbs, and If/Then Dynamics

Earth is stable until it isn't.

It's mountains, unmoving and eternal **until tectonic plates decide otherwise.** It's a stone wall, solid and sure, **until the mortar cracks and crumbles.** It's homeostasis—routine, predictability—**until a tiny, almost imperceptible shift tilts everything in a new direction.**

This is the nature of storytelling. You build something stable—a setting, a character, a moment of calm—so that when you disrupt it, the change **means something.**

This is why **if/then dynamics** matter.

If things remain the same, the story doesn't move. **But introduce one small disruption—just a single shift in the ground beneath your character's feet—and suddenly, the then is inevitable.**

It doesn't have to be a car crash, a gunshot, a storm rolling in. It can be something so small it almost goes unnoticed.

- *A cough that wasn't there yesterday.*
- *A glance that lingers just a little too long.*
- *A slight hesitation before answering a question.*

The reader might not even notice at first. But the story does. And **the ground has already begun to shift.**

Anecdotes of Disruption in the Earth Element

My friend, poet, and storyteller Jennifer Lighty had one of these moments.

She was free-swimming in Hawaiian waters when she felt something brush against her. A **shark.**

It was quick. Almost nothing. A flicker of movement, a passing shadow, there and gone in an instant.

But it **changed everything.**

Her book, *Pico, A Return to the Dreaming*, unfolds in the wake of that moment. A single, fleeting disruption—so small it could have been dismissed—**reshaped her entire creative trajectory.**

It doesn't take much. A ripple on the surface. A hairline fracture in stone.

Even my own work with stone walls has shown me this: **you imagine the structure before you build it, but the materials will always dictate the final shape.** You think you're stacking neat, uniform blocks, but reality hands you jagged edges, uneven weight, and stones that don't fit the way you thought they would.

The wall you envisioned? **It doesn't exist.**

But the one you build? **That's real.**

Nature as Our Greatest Teacher

Look outside. Watch the way the earth moves, the way it **doesn't.**

Mountains form in silence over lifetimes. Rivers carve through rock with patient insistence. Even in stillness, **change is happening.**

The same is true for your story.

It doesn't have to start with a crash. Maybe it starts with a whisper. Maybe it starts with **one ordinary moment—except for one tiny, almost imperceptible detail that shifts everything.**

Maybe it's:

- *A family dinner, everyone eating as usual—except the mother hasn't spoken once.*

- *A town, quiet and sleepy—except there's a new sound at night, just barely audible.*

- *A person going about their usual day—except they keep seeing the same stranger in different places.*

The disruption doesn't have to be **big.** It just has to exist.

Navigating Creative Blocks with Earth Dynamics

The hardest thing about writing is that **you know the whole story in your head, but the reader doesn't.**

What feels obvious to you might be invisible to them. What feels subtle to you might hit like a freight train.

That's why **breadcrumbs matter.**

You have to **leave enough clues** so your reader can follow, but not so many that the path is obvious. It's a balancing act. And the only way to get good at it? **Practice.**

Think about the last time your world—big or small—was upended. Not in a way that made headlines. Not in a way that other people necessarily noticed. **But in a way, that changed you.**

Maybe:

- You woke up and realized you no longer wanted the life you'd built.

- You heard a single sentence that reframed something you thought was solid.

- You saw something you weren't supposed to see.

Write about that moment. **Capture the stillness before the shift. The thing that seemed stable. The moment it cracked.**

Don't explain it. Don't justify it. Just **let the earth move.**

An Invitation to Build Your Foundation

Here's what I want you to do.

Take a moment. Find stillness. Feel the ground under your feet.

Then, let it shake—just a little.

- Write about something solid. A structure. A belief. A relationship.

- Introduce a shift. A disruption. A small crack in the foundation.

- Follow the change. Let it move where it wants to go.

The Earth element isn't about chaos. It's about **creating stability just long enough for its inevitable disruption to mean something.**

It's about **setting the stage for the if. Then, letting the then take over.**

Welcome to the Grounding Force

This is the first step. The first layer. The foundation.

But even now, even as we plant our feet in the dirt, we know something is coming.

The ground does not stay still forever.

Let's begin.

Chapter 2: Water – The Flow of Intuition

The ocean doesn't ask where you're going. It just **moves.**

One moment, you're floating—weightless, timeless—buoyed by the gentle pulse of the tide. The next, you're spinning, disoriented, a mouthful of salt and sand grinding between your teeth. The same wave that carried you forward **drags you under and tumbles you through a washing machine of pure kinetic force.** And then, just as suddenly, it spits you back out.

Water doesn't care about your plans.

And neither does your creativity.

The Wave: A Metaphor for Creative Flow

I love swimming in the ocean naked. It's not rebellion; it's **returning to the source.**

Humans are mostly water. The ocean is mostly salt. We match.

I've spent hours floating, letting the tide rock me, my body dissolving into the rhythm of something older than thought. I've written poems from underwater, imagined whole stories from beneath the surface, staring up at the way light fractures and bends.

But body surfing—that's where the real lesson is. **Catching a wave is pure intuition.**

- *Too early?* You miss the moment, the wave rolls past, and you're left bobbing uselessly in its wake.

- *Too late?* The wave doesn't carry you—it **owns you.** It flips you inside out, grinds you against the ocean floor, feeds you a few mouthfuls of sand just to remind you who's in charge.

The only way to ride it? **You have to feel it coming.**

You don't control the wave. You don't tell it when to break. You **listen**—and when the moment is right, you throw yourself forward and let it carry you.

Creativity is the same way.

The best ideas don't **obey you.** They don't arrive on a schedule. They **build**—somewhere deep, unseen, gathering momentum—until, all at once, they crest.

Miss the moment, and the energy dissipates. Try to force it, and you get wrecked.

But if you **time it right**, if you trust the pull—**you fly.**

Emotional Currents: The Dance of Intuition and Confusion

Water is intuition.

It's **that voice that whispers, "This way."** The quiet knowing. The gut feeling. The chill up your spine before something happens.

It's also **confusing.**

Because what is confusion, if not an undercurrent, pulling you in unexpected directions?

There's a myth that creativity should always feel good, like a pure, unbroken flow. But **anyone who's done this long enough knows that confusion is part of the process.**

I had a friend once tell me, *"If you're not confused, you're not diving deep enough."*

He was right.

Every time I've ever started writing something real—something that meant something—I've **hit a wall.**

The idea begins as clear as glass. **And then the fog rolls in.**

- *You start second-guessing yourself.*

- *You suddenly don't know if any of it makes sense.*

- *You feel like you're drowning in half-formed thoughts and contradictions.*

Good. That means **you're getting somewhere.**

Confusion isn't failure. Confusion is **movement.** The mind stirs up the silt at the bottom and clouds the water—**because something is shifting.**

And if you can sit with it—if you can let the current take you without fighting it—you'll break through.

Because just beyond confusion? **Clarity.**

Narrative Fluidity: Letting Your Story Flow Naturally

Some stories move like rivers—winding, meandering, always seeking a path forward. Others crash like waves—**short bursts of momentum, moments of stillness before the next surge.**

Your job isn't to **force** it. It's to **follow the flow.**

I learned this the hard way.

Back in college, I had an editor who—whenever I turned in an article—would skim it, nod, and say, "**There's nothing inherently interesting about the ignorant becoming slightly less ignorant.**"

I had no idea what he meant at first.

Then it hit me.

He was telling me: **Stop writing as if the answers matter more than the questions.** Stop pretending you've got everything figured out. Let the uncertainty show.

Let the story move the way it wants.

Intuition in Writing: Tapping into Your Subconscious

Creativity doesn't **live in your frontal lobe.**

It doesn't come from the part of your brain that calculates, analyzes, and double-checks every detail. It comes from **the deep places—** from whatever subconscious reservoir holds **everything you've ever seen, heard, felt, and forgotten.**

If Earth is the place where we build, structure and plan, Water is **where we surrender.**

How do you tap into it?

- **Freewrite.** No editing. No stopping. Let your brain spill onto the page before your inner critic can wake up.

- **Write underwater.** (Or at least imagine you are.) Feel the weightlessness. Let the words drift, shift, ripple.

- **Follow the thread.** That weird, unexpected sentence that appears in the middle of a paragraph? That's the storytelling **you where it wants to go.**

When I write, I trust the undercurrents. I don't **force** the wave—I **wait for it.**

Balancing Intuition and Confusion: The Yin and Yang of Water

If creativity were only about intuition—only about perfect clarity—we'd never grow.

But **the ocean isn't just glassy surfaces and gentle tides.**

It's rip currents. Undertows. Tsunamis.

It's days when you dive in expecting warmth, and instead, **the cold punches the air from your lungs.**

Confusion is the storm before the stillness.

You **need both.**

- *Intuition is knowing where the current is taking you.*
- *Confusion is what happens when you fight against it.*

So don't fight it. **Float.**

A Personal Invitation to Embrace the Flow

Here's what I want you to do.

- **Write a moment of clarity.**

- **Then disrupt it.**

Maybe:

- A child walking along a shoreline, collecting seashells—until they find **something else.**

- A woman staring out at a still lake, lost in thought—until **a single ripple** breaks the reflection.

- A conversation that starts **smooth, easy, and effortless—until one sentence changes everything.**

Describe the **flow.** Then, introduce the wave that **knocks everything off balance.**

A Final Reflection on the Water Element

Creativity **isn't static.** It moves. It **has to move.**

It **lifts us**—and it **tosses us.**

Sometimes, we hydroplane, skimming effortlessly across the surface. Other times, we **wipe out completely**, crash into the surf, get tumbled against the ocean floor, and walk away with sand in our teeth.

Both are necessary.

Both are Water.

So wade in. Let the current take you. **And when the next wave comes, catch it.**

Chapter 3: Fire – The Spark of Passion

Flames flicker, stories burn. The night hums with electricity, a storm of words waiting to ignite. You've felt it before—that moment when everything aligns, when the idea isn't just an idea anymore but a **force**. Fire is the moment of combustion. **The strike of a match in the dark.** The thing that drives you forward so fast you barely have time to second-guess.

But fire is never just **one thing**. It **creates and destroys, lights the way, and consumes the path behind it.** Passion and obsession? Same flame, different burn.

And that's what we're here to explore.

Igniting the Narrative: From Water's Flow to Fire's Flame

Picture this: You've just pulled yourself out of the **cool, shifting currents of Water**—intuition, confusion, deep-sea exploration. You're drenched, blinking in the sun, and **then it happens**—a **spark**. The idea clarifies, crackling into form.

It's like catching the first scent of smoke in the air before you even see the fire. You don't **think**—you **feel** it. The certainty, the momentum. The moment you know exactly what your story wants to be.

Fire doesn't wait for permission. It doesn't **hesitate**.

This is where the if/then dynamic returns. If Water was about floating, following, and allowing the current to take you wherever it wanted, **then Fire is the moment of decision.** The part where you stop waiting and **take the reins.** It's the undeniable surge forward.

If the **passion is true,** it carries you. If the **fire burns too hot,** it consumes.

***

The Dual Nature of Fire: Passion Versus Obsession

A controlled burn clears deadwood and makes room for new growth. A wildfire devours everything in its path.

This is the line Fire forces us to walk—between **fueling the flame** and **letting it rage unchecked.**

Consider the **house on fire** metaphor. You wake up, smoke curling under the door. The flames lick the walls. In the lowest state of instinct, **you run blindly out of fear.** Maybe you leap over someone in your way—maybe you don't even notice them. The fire **owns you.**

In a higher instinctive state? **You still run. But you grab the ones you love, you think beyond the immediate burn, you make choices.**

Same fire. **Different results.**

Harold in *Harold and Maude* didn't just **love** Maude. He loved her with a **fury.** A passion that **transformed** him. That's a fire in its highest form—the kind that lights you up from within, reminds you that you're alive, shakes the dust off your bones, and makes you see the world in an entirely new way.

Then there's the other kind.

Think of **the worst decisions in human history**. Wars. Betrayals. The destruction of entire civilizations. **Passion twisted into obsession**. People were convinced they were acting on the highest ideals when, really, they were burning everything to the ground because they couldn't tell the difference between **fueling the fire and being consumed by it**.

Fire transforms. Fire destroys. Same flame.

Personal Reflections: Instinct, Passion, and the Human Heart

I've felt Fire's pull in my own work.

That moment when you hit **the perfect phrase,** the exact image, and your hands move faster than your thoughts when your characters stop feeling like **inventions** and start moving with their own volition. **When you are no longer creating but transcribing.**

That's **Fire at its best.**

I've also felt **the other side.**

The moments when I've gotten **too lost in the heat of it.** When I've written with so much intensity that I couldn't see **the tunnel vision forming around me**. When I've **clung too hard** to an idea, too sure that this—this thing—was the most important thing I'd ever create, until I realized I'd been circling the same inferno for **weeks, months, maybe even years.**

The difference? **Fire, at its best, moves forward. Fire at its worst keeps you trapped.**

It's the line between **passion and fixation, inspiration and self-destruction.**

Toggling Between Extremes: When Passion Spurs Progress

Fire is the moment when your characters stop wandering and start **wanting** something.

- *The love that won't be denied.*

- *The revenge that has to happen, no matter the cost.*

- *The hunger that makes them climb, fight, and burn their way forward.*

It's **the drive that pushes the narrative beyond comfort.**

But what happens when **passion flips to obsession?**

- *The love that becomes possession.*

- *The revenge that consumes everything in its path.*

- *The hunger that hollows out the person who once carried it.*

This is where Fire creates the **greatest stories**—not just **want** but the **cost of want.** Not just passion, but **the consequences when passion burns too hot.**

Practical Wisdom: Embracing the Flame Without Getting Burned

1. Recognize the Surge

When the fire **hits**, ride it. Don't overthink, don't hesitate—**write until the momentum slows.**

2. Step Back Before the Burnout

If you find yourself **obsessing** over a single scene, sentence, or idea—pause. Walk away. Breathe. Let the fire settle so you can see **if you're still creating or if you're just fanning the flames.**

3. Find the Heat in Your Characters

Who in your story is **on fire**? What drives them? What are they willing to burn for? **What happens when that heat spirals beyond their control?**

A Writing Exercise: Ignite and Tame the Flame

Set a timer for **ten minutes.**

Write a scene where a character is **on fire for something**—love, revenge, ambition, a desperate need. **Make it visceral.** Let the passion burn on the page.

Then—twist it.

Push that passion **past the breaking point.** Where does it go? What does it cost? Does it lift them higher, or does it consume them?

End the scene **with a choice: feed the fire or extinguish it.**

Final Reflections on the Fire Element

We are made of fire.

It fuels us, lifts us, **makes us move.**

It is the part of us that **knows what it wants**—and the part of us that forgets everything else in pursuit of it.

When balanced, Fire is the force that **makes us come alive.** When unchecked, Fire is the thing that **destroys everything in its path.**

Know when to stoke the flames.
Know when to step back.
Know when to let something **burn away so something else can rise.**

Because this—**this is where stories transform.**

Chapter 4: Wind – The Breath of Change

The wind shifts, and suddenly, everything is different. One minute, you're coasting, catching the breeze like a paper lantern drifting through an autumn sky. The next, you're walking around a corner in New York, and a wet plastic bag slaps you in the face. **The wind is unpredictable.** It's the element of sudden realization, of seeing beyond yourself, of feeling your narrative start to exist **outside of you**—no longer just a private thing, but something beginning to take shape in the world.

This is the moment in the process when we **look up**. We've built the foundation on Earth, waded through the emotional currents of Water, and let the Fire surge and burn in our chests. And now, **we turn outward**. The wind is perspective. The wind is movement. Wind is **love and fixation, clarity and obsession, the push and pull between freedom and attachment.**

The Winds of Change: When Perspective Shifts

There's a reason ancient myths associate the wind with **messages from the gods**. Wind whispers things we didn't know we needed to hear. It carries ideas from unseen places and drops unexpected seeds into the soil of our stories. **A sudden breeze, a new angle, a shift in perspective—and suddenly, the story isn't just yours anymore.**

Here, in the wind, is where we start asking the bigger questions:

- *How does this story live beyond me?*

- *Where does my narrative fit within the larger world of stories?*

- *How will this be received?*

But just like any force of nature, **wind doesn't always arrive as a gentle guiding hand.** Sometimes, it sweeps in with the violence of a storm, and suddenly, everything you thought was solid is **uprooted and flying sideways.**

This is where love and fixation begin their dangerous dance.

Love vs. Fixation: The Tornado Effect

The wind is love. The way it moves through us, how it **connects one thing to another, one person to another.** It's how a story starts to breathe—how it **expands, adapts, and interacts with the world around it.** When we love a story, we let it move; we **let it be alive.**

But fixation? Fixation is the hurricane.

In the same way, **Fire toggles between passion and obsession, Wind carries the potential for both love and fixation.** At its best, **wind is freedom**—the ability to let go, to release, to watch something grow and transform beyond what we imagined. But when that energy gets too intense, too controlled, **we start gripping too tightly.** We demand it takes a certain shape and refuses to let it be affected by outside forces.

That's where stories get **stale.**

Ever had that moment where you refuse to let go of an idea, **even though you know it's not working?** That's wind-turned-tornado. A love for your narrative that has **morphed into a storm of control.** A refusal to let it exist outside of what you imagined in the beginning.

Real love? **Real love lets things change.**

Think about characters in love. The good ones. The ones who pulse with energy. Their love isn't just still water. **It moves, it shifts, and it collides with obstacles. It doesn't own—it evolves.**

The stories that **cling too tightly**—whether in narrative structure, character arcs, or thematic elements—become **fixations** instead of living, breathing entities. **A story locked in a glass case instead of one running free through the streets.**

The Circular Nature of Wind: Outside-In, Inside-Out

Wind doesn't move in straight lines. **It circles, it loops, it revisits ideas in new ways.**

When we're deep in the Fire element, we're **pushing outward**—projecting, declaring, and making decisions. But in Wind, **we start to look back in**, viewing what we've built with fresh eyes.

There's a concept in storytelling—call it the **Jewel Center**, call it the **Bhagwa**, call it **whatever you want**—but it works like this:

1.	**Find the heart of your story.** The glowing ember in the middle of it all.

2.	**Circle around it.** Approach it from every possible angle. See how it changes depending on where you're standing.

3.	**Let it breathe.** If you stare at it too hard, you're fixated. If you ignore it, the wind takes it away. **Balance.**

Jack Kerouac used this method, writing into the **core** of his ideas from every possible side until something **clicked**. Wind isn't about control. It's about **movement**, about **letting go just enough to let your story find its own rhythm.**

Write Like the Wind: Speed, Experimentation, and Letting Go

Here's something about the Wind element: it moves **fast.**

This is where we start to **write without overthinking.** The time for careful, deliberate construction is later. Right now, we're moving with the story, **letting the wind take us where it wants.**

Exercise: The Wind Sprint

1. Set a timer for **ten minutes.**

2. Pick a scene, a concept, a moment—**anything you've been circling for too long.**

3. Write it **fast.** No stopping, no overthinking. Let the words spill out like wind ripping through an open window.

If you stall, **repeat this to yourself:**

I am the wind. I am moving. I am writing. I do not stop.

The goal isn't perfection. It's **speed, movement, seeing where the wind takes you.**

When the Wind Settles: Perspective, Humor, and Reflection

Not every gust of wind is a **tornado of existential realization.** Sometimes, Wind is **humor**—the sudden moment of levity in a serious scene, the shift in tone that saves a narrative from being too one-note.

Wind allows us to **laugh at ourselves**, to acknowledge when we're taking things too seriously, and to let in the unexpected. If every element so far has been **deeply personal**, Wind is the moment we **step outside of ourselves** and see the bigger picture.

It's perspective. It's the moment when we stop saying *This is my story* and start saying *How does this story live beyond me?*

Final Thoughts on Wind: Letting the Story Take Flight

If Earth is our foundation, Water is our intuition, and Fire is our momentum, then Wind is **what carries the story into the world**.

The wind is love, connection, and **letting go.**
The wind is **fixation, obsession, a refusal to release.**

It is both.

And our job? Our job is to **navigate the difference.**

To let the wind carry us, but not let it **own us.**
To love a story but **not suffocate it.**
To let the gusts **shake things loose** but not let them **tear it all apart.**

The wind is the breath in the story's lungs. **Let it breathe.**

Chapter 5: The Void – Bozos on the Bus with Infinite Potential

The Void. The space between molecules. The breath between thoughts. The moment before the curtain rises or the final note fades into silence. It's everything and nothing. The place where **our stories either fuse into something undeniable or begin to quietly, inexorably unravel.**

But let's be clear—**the Void is not a vacuum.** It's not an empty abyss, some nihilistic black hole where meaning goes to die. No, the Void is the place where **everything lives at once.** It's the realm of infinite potential, where ideas flicker in and out of existence, waiting for us to **catch them, shape them, or let them slip back into the ether.**

This is the final stage of the process, but it's not the end. Not even close. **It's just another beginning.**

Bozos on the Bus with the Potential for the Infinite

A friend of mine used to love saying, *"We're just Bozos on the bus."* You know, that classic line about how none of us really know what we're doing, that we're all just bumbling along through existence, trying our best to make sense of it all.

I used to nod and then, with a smirk, flip it on its head:

"We're Bozos on the bus... with the potential for the infinite."

It was fun watching his mind explode with that one.

Because that's the Void, that's what we're doing here. **We are all Bozos on the bus, but at any moment, we can tap into something limitless.** At any moment, the right story, the right phrase, and the right shift in perspective can open up an entire **universe** of meaning.

Think of it like this: **every story ever told, every song ever sung, every invention, every poem, every work of art—everything that has ever existed—was pulled from this same infinite well.** Some ideas slip through our fingers. Others, we catch and shape. But they all come from the same place.

And here's the wild part: **this process doesn't stop.**

You finish a story, and what happens? **Another one begins.**

Spielberg had it right when he said, *"A story isn't about finishing—it's about beginning, and then beginning again."*

The Void as a Space of Infinite Markings

If Earth is **solid reality**, Water is **fluid emotion**, Fire is **driving passion**, and Wind is **shifting perspective**, then **the Void is where you recognize the pattern beneath them all.**

This is where you finally **see the full shape of what you've created.** The moment when the mosaic pulls together, when every fragment, every beat, every element interlocks into something that makes sense—not just as separate parts, but as a whole.

Or maybe it doesn't.

Maybe you step back and see **cracks.** Inconsistencies. Threads you thought would lead somewhere but just… don't.

That's the Void, too.

It's the place where everything either locks into place **or begins to fray at the edges.**

It's where you decide **what holds and what doesn't.** What is worth keeping, refining, and elevating—and what is already **starting to decay, crumbling even as you hold it?**

There's a passage in the *I Ching* about reaching the end of a cycle, where things have been developed to the degree they can be. The warning? Without vigilance, **decline is inevitable.** That's the other truth of the Void—**synthesis and decay are always dancing together.**

And yet, here's the paradox: **even decay is just another form of creation.**

Because what happens when things start to break down?

We begin again.

The Narrative Cycle: Beginning Anywhere, Returning as Needed

A story doesn't need to **start at the beginning.** Sometimes, it starts right here, in the Void, fully formed, and we work our way **backward** to find the missing pieces.

Some stories **ignite in Fire**, a burst of raw, creative energy that has to be sculpted into something coherent. Some emerge **in the shifting winds**, an idea circling our minds before it finally finds its place. Others rise **from deep waters**, intuitive and emotional, only revealing their full meaning later.

No matter **where** your story begins, know this: **you can always return to fill in what's missing.**

You don't have to build everything in order.

If your story arrives in the Void, **trust it.** Follow it. **Let it lead you.** You can return to Earth for structure, to Water for emotional depth, to Fire for passion, and to Wind for perspective.

Everything is connected. Every element feeds into the next.

Synthesis or Degradation: What Holds and What Cracks?

The Void asks a simple but brutal question:

Is this working?

Is your story coming together into something undeniable? Or is there a creeping sense of **disintegration**—loose ends that don't resolve, emotional beats that don't land, a theme that once felt powerful but now rings hollow?

If it's solid? Run with it.

If it's **cracking at the seams?** Don't panic.

Stories resist synthesis sometimes. It doesn't mean they're broken. It just means they **need to cycle back through the elements** before they're ready. Maybe the emotions need more depth. Maybe the structure needs tightening. Maybe you **need to burn part of it down and start again.**

That's not failure. That's **creation.**

Tools of the Void: Freedom and Flexibility

The Void is the great humbler.

It reminds us that every formula, every writing rule, every so-called universal truth about storytelling is **just a tool**.

Three-act structure? Useful.
 Four-act structure? Also useful.
 The Hero's Journey? Great, if it fits.
 Throwing structure out the window and letting instinct lead? That works, too.

The Void lets you **choose the tools that serve your story** and discard the ones that don't.

Master a few first—**five elements, five tools.** Understand them deeply. Then, as you go, **add more.**

But never let a tool **dictate the story**. The story always comes first.

Mini-Exercise: A Monologue at the Edge of Knowing

Write a **monologue** from the perspective of a character standing at the brink of synthesis.

They are seeing the **whole picture** for the first time. Every memory, every choice, every moment leading to this singular **realization.**

But then—**introduce a crack.**

One line. One small doubt. One whisper of entropy, creeping in at the edges.

"I stand here, the sum of everything I've ever been. Everything lines up; every thread weaves through me, every moment, every choice, leading here. And yet—there is something beneath my feet. A shift. A silence. The faint sound of something unraveling."

Write **into** that tension. Feel the Void **as both infinite possibility and quiet disintegration.**

Final Reflections on the Void: The Art of Beginning Again

Every ending **is just another doorway.**

The Void is not about **finality.** It's about knowing that **there is always another cycle, another story, another beginning.**

Your job, as a writer, isn't to **finish.** It's to recognize when something is whole and when something still needs to be discovered.

We are all Bozos on the bus. But we are Bozos on the bus **with the potential for the infinite.**

Welcome to the Void.

It's never empty. It's just waiting.

Here's your enhanced chapter, fully immersed in your style—where narrative momentum isn't just about structure but about riding the pulse of the fictive dream.

Chapter 6: Integrating the Elements – Navigating Narrative Momentum

Somewhere between the stability of Earth and the infinite potential of the Void, there is motion. A pulse. A beat. The rhythm of a story not just existing, but moving—**propelled by the push and pull of opposing forces, the interplay of grounded certainty and chaotic expansion.**

This is where narrative momentum lives.

At this point, you've gathered the tools, tapped into the elements, and started seeing how they work together. But how do you **keep it all in motion?** How do you **balance the forces without getting stuck in one place, without losing the pulse that makes a story feel alive?**

Think of it like a dance—**sometimes you lead, sometimes you follow, and sometimes you simply feel the rhythm.**

The Elemental Dance

Picture a grand ballroom, each element taking the floor in turn.

Earth arrives first, steady and unshakable, laying the foundation. The deep, grounding drumbeat of your story. **The world that holds your characters. The rules that govern them.**

Water follows fluid and shifting. The violin swells, the movement of emotion across a character's face, the moments when the story ebbs and flows between clarity and uncertainty.

Fire leaps into the center, wild and untamed. The brass section. The pulse of conflict, passion, and drive that **pushes the story forward**—sometimes too fast, sometimes reckless, sometimes beautiful.

Then Wind—unpredictable, playful, sharp. It changes direction without warning, spinning the dancers and shifting perspectives. A gust that alters the landscape, an insight that changes everything.

And finally, the Void. The moment when **all these energies meet and fold into each other.** The space where the dance becomes something else—something whole and complete, yet still reaching for the next step, the next cycle.

Because the story doesn't stop, even when it ends, it begins again.

Where Do You Start? Anywhere.

You don't have to start with Earth. You don't have to **begin at the beginning.** Some stories **erupt into being** from Fire—**a moment of obsession, of fierce drive, a scene that won't leave you alone.** Others emerge in the deep waters of intuition, pulling you in before you even know what you're writing about. Some swirl in the Wind, fragmented, unpredictable, landing where they choose before taking off again.

Start where the energy is, wherever that may be.

Then, work backwards. **Fill in the missing pieces.**

The Void doesn't care if you built your story in order. It only cares that the pieces—however, scattered, however chaotic—**eventually find each other.**

Finding Balance: The Energy at Play

Momentum is **not** about speed. It's about **sustained motion**. That means balance. That means knowing **when to push, when to pull, when to accelerate, and when to pause.**

Ask yourself:

- **Earth:** Is your foundation strong? Can the reader trust the world you've built? Do the characters **feel real, tethered to something stable, even if the ground later shakes beneath them?**

- **Water:** Are emotions flowing naturally? Do your characters' choices ripple through the story? Or are they dammed up, blocked, or held back when they need to move?

- **Fire:** What's **pushing** your narrative forward? What **burns** inside your characters? Is passion driving them, or are they on the edge of obsession, losing control?

- **Wind:** Are you allowing the story to breathe? Are surprises sweeping through, clearing the air, shaking things up? Or is the air **stagnant**, choking under the weight of predictability?

- **The Void:** Can you see it all now? The synthesis? Or are cracks forming—signs of decay creeping in, telling you it's time to begin again?

Shifting Perspective: The Narrative Doesn't Belong to You Alone

This is where things change.

Up until now, you've been inside the story. **Inside your head, inside your characters, inside the fictive dream.** But at some point, you have to step outside of it.

The wind is here again, whispering in your ear.

A story isn't just what you see—it's what others see. The moment you step back and view it from the outside, the shape shifts. What made perfect sense from the inside suddenly has gaps. What felt clear becomes tangled. What was powerful in your head might not **yet** translate onto the page.

This is **not** failure. This is **the next step.**

At this stage, **it's not just your story anymore.** It's a conversation.

The energy shifts from **"What do I want to say?"** to **"How is this being received?"** From **"What does this mean to me?"** to **"What does this mean when it leaves me?"**

This is **the wind turning into a storm**—circling the story, picking up loose threads, **forcing you to look from every possible angle.**

Mini-Exercise: Weaving the Elements into a Narrative

Let's map it out.

Start with **a central idea**—the *Jewel Center.* **One single truth, one theme, one burning question that pulses at the heart of your story.**

Then, layer the elements in.

- **Earth:** Establish stability. What's the grounding force in your story? Is it the setting? A character's core belief? The foundation before the inevitable disruption?

- **Water:** Where does emotion flow? What moment shifts from clarity to confusion? Where does **intuition guide action?**

- **Fire:** The moment everything ignites. The turning point. **What happens that can't be undone?**

- **Wind:** The change. The shift in perspective. **Where does the unexpected force its way in?** What disrupts, what challenges, and what pushes the story into a new current?

- **The Void:** Synthesis or decay? **What holds? What falls apart?** What question lingers, refusing to be fully answered?

Final Thoughts: The Motion Never Stops

There's no single way to **navigate** a story. No perfect structure. No absolute roadmap.

The only real rule? **Keep it moving.**

When something **stalls**, change the energy. If the **groundwork feels stuck**, shake it up with Wind. If emotions **aren't landing**, deepen the Water. If the **passion is missing**, bring in Fire. If things are too **chaotic**, return to Earth. If the whole thing **feels ready, but something's off**, look to the Void.

Momentum is never about **forcing** a story forward. It's about **knowing how to shift the energy when it starts to fade.**

Writing is a dance. Sometimes you lead, sometimes you follow, **sometimes you just close your eyes and let the music take you.**

So, step onto the floor.

Find the pulse.

And **keep moving.**

Here's your enhanced version, fully in your style—where the prompts aren't just starting points but cracks in reality, where the flickering neon of the fictive dream is always one breath away from becoming a wildfire.

Writing Prompts & Exercises: Working with the Elements

Crickets and locusts are the squeaky wheels of summer. The river moves left when you expect it to move right. Someone knocks at the door. Nobody is there.

You write a scene expecting it to go one way, and instead, it drifts, turns, burns, and evaporates. **That's the point.**

These prompts are a place to start, not a place to stay. Pick one, write into it, and then—when the ground shakes, when the wind picks up—**see where it leads.**

Earth – Laying the Foundation and Breaking It

Stable Ground Prompt

Write a scene that establishes an unshakable world. Focus on concrete details—setting, character traits, and daily routines. Then, introduce a small but noticeable disruption. A flickering lightbulb, a knock at the door, a dog barking at nothing.

Sudden Explosion Prompt

Describe something that seems solid and unchangeable. Then, flip it—introduce an unexpected force that causes it to collapse, erode, or transform. A mountain crumbles. A relationship fractures. A simple truth turns out to be a lie.

Worldbuilding Exercise

Spend 10 minutes writing about a place that feels permanent, structured, and real. Now, imagine a disruption—an external force, a secret hidden in its foundation, or a slow but inevitable shift.

Water – The Flow Between Intuition and Confusion

Stream of Consciousness Prompt

Set a timer for 10 minutes and write nonstop about something abstract—love, fear, memory, loss. Don't filter yourself. Then, go back and underline the first line that truly feels right. That's your starting point—everything before was just finding your way there.

Intuition vs. Confusion Prompt

Write a scene where a character is guided by an intuitive sense of what's right. Then, introduce an event or revelation that throws them into doubt. **Do they regain clarity or sink further into confusion?**

Sensory Detail Exercise

Describe water in as many states as possible—flowing, still, crashing, evaporating. Then, translate that movement into an emotional arc.

Fire – The Thin Line Between Passion and Obsession

Passion Ignition Prompt

Write a monologue from a character who has just discovered something they're deeply passionate about. Let their enthusiasm spill onto the page.

The Obsession Flip Prompt

Take that same passion and push it into obsession. **What happens when they lose control?** What do they sacrifice in pursuit of their goal?

The Line Game Exercise

Freewrite passionately about any subject for a set time. When done, go back and underline the first line that truly hits. **That's where your real story starts. Everything before? Just warming up.**

Wind – The Movement Between Love and Fixation

Love tilts toward hate. The same breeze that cools the skin can peel it away.

Wind doesn't just move—it pushes. It turns a whisper into a scream, a glance into an obsession. Wind is the space where love becomes something else, where change is inevitable but never predictable.

Love into Fixation Prompt

Write about a character experiencing deep, genuine love for something—an idea, a person, a place. Then, introduce a shift. **How does their love become a fixation? How do they try to rationalize it?**

Dialogue and Change Prompt

Write a conversation between two people where one is ready for change and the other resists it. Let the dialogue flow naturally. **Does the change occur, or does the resistance hold?**

Character Perspective Flip Exercise

Take a character you've written before. Now, write a scene from the perspective of someone who sees them in a completely different light. **Let this shift change the tone and perception of the story.**

Final Thoughts: The Invitation to Keep Moving

If there's one thing to take away from this process, it's that **the journey doesn't stop.**

Writing isn't about "figuring it out" once and for all—it's about continuing to walk, **one foot in front of the other, watching how the landscape shifts.** Some days, the elements move in perfect harmony. On other days, they crash against each other, **creating unexpected collisions.**

That's the beauty of it.

So, use these prompts, but don't be bound by them. Use the elements, but don't compartmentalize them. **Every story, every moment, contains all five elements at once—you're just deciding where to focus.**

Final Challenge: Write the Shift

Before you close this book, try one thing:

Pick an element, any element, and write for five minutes. No stopping, no overthinking—just move with it. **See where it takes you.**

Then, when you're done, ask yourself: **What changed while you wrote?** Did the energy stay in one place, or did it shift?

Guards are selling explosives to the patients. **Things are really tricky.**

That's the process, right there.

The movement, the discovery, **the next step forward.**

And **that's what this is all about.**

Keep experimenting.

Keep chasing the wind, diving into the water, playing with fire, grounding yourself in the earth, and stepping into the vast openness of the void.

The fictive dream is an ongoing journey.

You already know this.

We are, perhaps, nibbling at the edges of being a failed state. Maybe more than nibbling. Maybe we've already choked down the first few bites. History has its rhythms, and one of them—the one that matters right now—is that when things break, when things fall, when the center collapses, and the roads lead nowhere, the only way out is through new stories.

That's the work. It has always been the work.

And the only way forward is to take that next step.

See you in the wind…